NATIONAL GEOGRAPHIC

PROPERTY OF
N.Y.C. Department of Education
Title I ARRA

Time Lines: 1900–2000

D1369893

Liam Collins

PROPERTY OF
N.Y.C. Department of Education
Title I ARRA

Things Change Over Time

Think about a typical day. Did you ride in a car? Did you watch television? Did you play a game on a computer? These are things kids do all the time. But this wasn't always true.

Kids living long ago couldn't do many of the things you do. They didn't have televisions or computers. Life long ago wasn't the same as it is today. That's because things change over time.

These photos show things kids did for fun long ago.

Time Lines

One way to show change over time is to use a time line. A time line shows important events in the order in which they happened. How do you read a time line? It's easy.

The time line below shows events in a girl's life. Start reading at the left. Look at the first date. This is where the time line begins. It begins with a baby being born.

Read the next date to the right to find out what happened next. "1995: Alia takes her first steps."

Alia is born.

| 1994 | 1995 | 1996 | 1997 |

Alia takes her first steps.

The space between the dates shows how much time has passed. The bigger the space, the more time between events. Alia started school four years after she took her first steps.

Now that you know how to read a time line let's find out how everyday life has changed over the past 100 years.

Alia starts school.

1999   2000   2001   2002

Alia learns to use
in-line skates.

1900–1920

What was life like a hundred years ago? It was a lot different from today. Many things that are common now didn't exist a hundred years ago. Electricity had been invented, but many people did not have it in their homes. Read the time line below to see a few of the things that happened between 1900–1920.

The Wright brothers built and flew the first airplane.

1900   1903   1905

The first movie theater opened in the United States.

Here are two more things that happened during this time period. Where would they go on the time line?

✳ 1903: First baseball World Series

✳ 1920: First regular radio broadcasts

Henry Ford used an assembly line to make low-priced cars.

1913 **1917** **1920**

The zipper was invented.

1920–1940

A lot of things changed over the next 20 years. Cities grew bigger. Cars became much more common. For fun people listened to radio shows. Television hadn't been invented yet. Read the time line below to see a few of the things that happened between 1920–1940.

The Band-Aid® was invented.

1920 **1925**

Packaged frozen food was sold for the first time.

Here are two more things that happened during this time period. Where would they go on the time line?

* 1928: Bubble gum invented
* 1930: Clear, sticky tape sold for first time

The Lone Ranger, a popular radio show, was first broadcast.

1933 **1937** **1940**

The first full-length cartoon movie opened.

1940–1960

During this time many people moved out of the cities and into the suburbs. Many people had electric appliances in their homes. Television became popular in the 1950s. Read the time line below to see a few of the things that happened between 1940–1960.

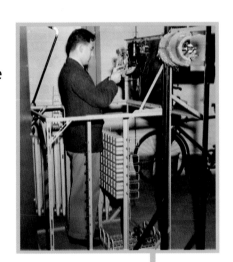

Scientists built the first computer.

1940 | 1946 | 1948

Velcro was invented.

Here are two more things that happened during this time period. Where would they go on the time line?

✳ 1942: First t-shirts made

✳ 1954: First shopping mall was built

Television shows were broadcast across the country for the first time.

1951 **1959** **1960**

Barbie® dolls were sold for the first time.

1960–1980

Your parents were probably kids during this time period. They grew up with color television. The personal computer was invented during this time, but most people did not have one. Read the time line below to see a few of the things that happened between 1960–1980.

Soda was sold in a can for the first time.

1960

1969

Astronaut Neil Armstrong became the first man to set foot on the moon.

Here are two more things that happened during this time period. Where would they go on the time line?

✷ 1967: First Super Bowl

✷ 1971: Disney World theme park opened

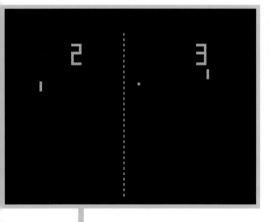

The first video game, Pong, was released.

1972 **1975** **1980**

The first personal computers were sold.

1980–2000

Computers changed daily life between 1980–2000, and computers still affect our lives. We live in a world that your great-grandparents couldn't have imagined. Read the time line below to see a few of the things that happened between 1980–2000.

Cordless phones were introduced.

1980 1981   1983

Music was recorded on compact discs (CDs) and sold in the United States for the first time.

Here are two more things that happened during this time period. Where would they go on the time line?

✳ 1980: Camcorder introduced

✳ 1990: First laptop computer sold

The Internet could be used on home computers.

1993 **2000**

The first crew lived in the International Space Station for four months.

2000–2100

What will a time line of the next 100 years look like?
What changes might you see? What will life be like
for your children? What will life be like 100 years
from now?

2000 ←————————————————————→ 2100